Music Minus One

4078

VERDI
OPERA ARIAS
FOR
BASS-BARITONE
WITH ORCHESTRA

MMO 4078

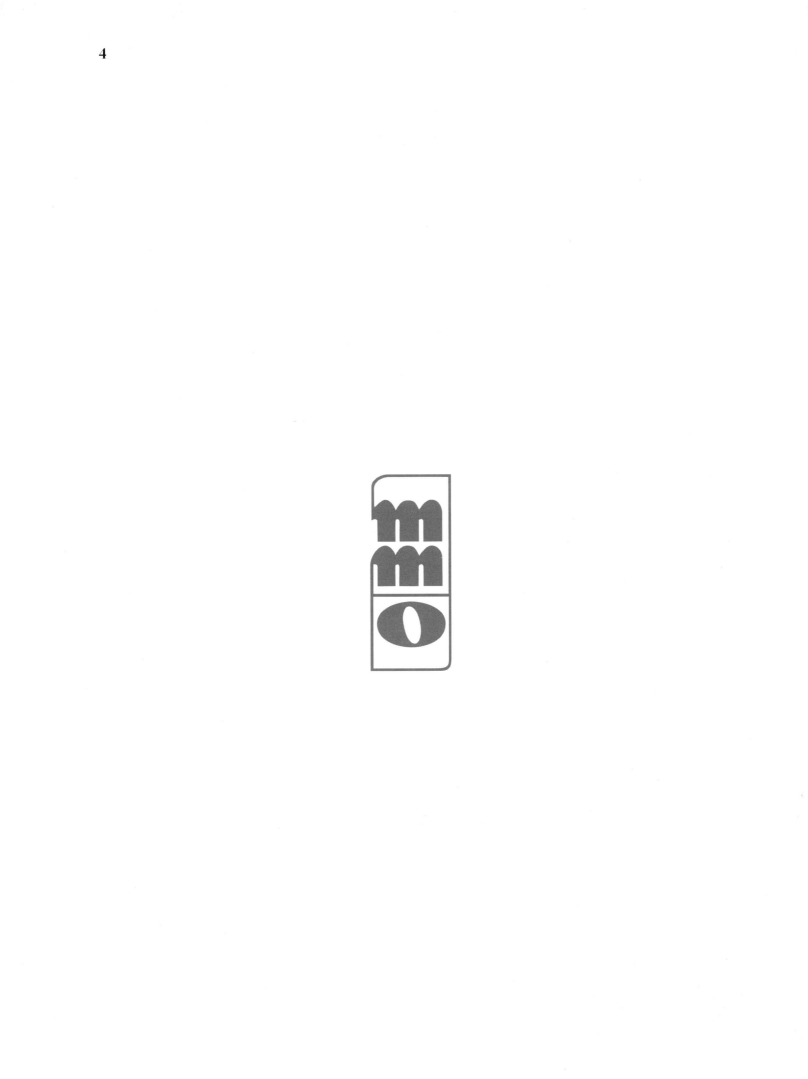

CDG
4078

Music Minus One Bass-Baritone

Verdi Opera Arias

for Bass-Baritone with Orchestra

SUGGESTIONS FOR USING THIS MMO EDITION

WE HAVE TRIED TO CREATE a product that will provide you an easy way to learn and perform these operatic arias with a full orchestra in the comfort of your own home. Because it involves a fixed orchestral performance, there is an inherent lack of flexibility in tempo and cadenza length. The following MMO features and techniques will reduce these inflexibilities and help you maximize the effectiveness of the MMO practice and performance system:

Regarding tempi: we have observed generally accepted tempi, but some may wish to perform at a different tempo, or to slow down or speed up the accompaniment for practice purposes. You can purchase from MMO (or from other audio and electronics dealers) A specialized CD player which allow variable speed while maintaining proper pitch. This is an indispensable tool for the serious musician and you may wish to look into purchasing this useful piece of equipment for full enjoyment of all your MMO editions.

We want to provide you with the most useful practice and performance accompaniments possible. If you have any suggestions for improving the MMO system, please feel free to contact us. You can reach us by e-mail at mmogroup@musicminusone.com.

Nabucco, Act II

"Vieni o Levita!...
...Tu sul labbro de veggenti"

Giuseppe Verdi
(1813-1901)

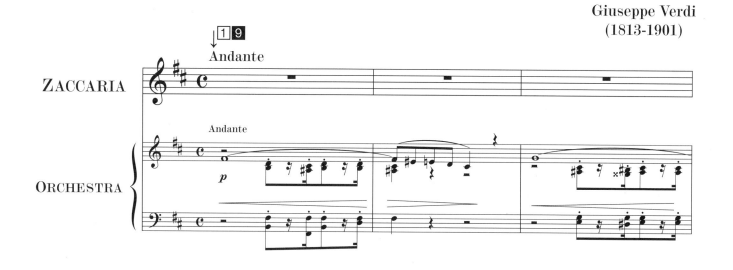

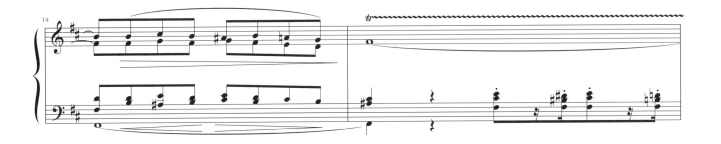

Recit.

Vie - ni,o Le - vi - ta!.. Il san - to co - di - ce

a tempo

re - ca! Di no - vel por - ten - - - to me

vuol mi - ni - stro Id - di - - - - - o!.. Me ser - vo

man - da, per glo - ria d'I - sra - el - le, le te - ne - bre a squar - ciar d'un in - fe -

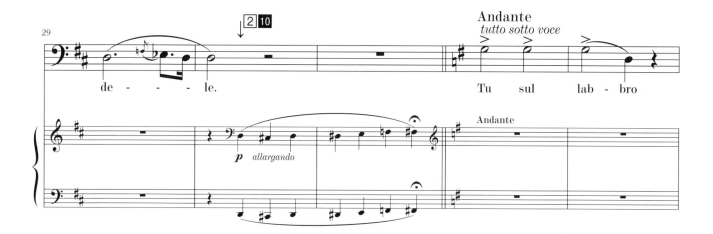

de - - le. Tu sul lab - bro

de' veg - gen - ti ful - mi - na - sti, o

som - mo... Id - di - o! All' As - si - ria in for - ti ac - cen - it par - la or

tu col lab - bro mi - o! E di can - ti e di

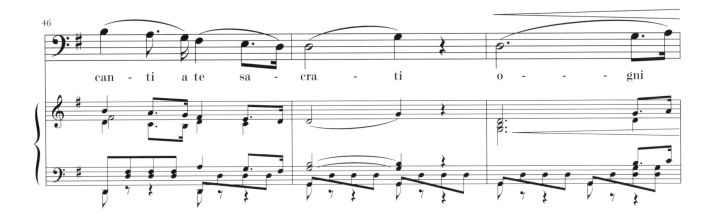

can - ti a te sa - cra - ti o - - - gni

tem - pio, o - gni tem - pio suo - ne - rà; so - vra

gl'i - do - li spez - za - - - ti la tua leg - ge sor - ge -

rà, so - vra gl'i - do - li spez - za - - ti la tua

leg - ge sor - - - ge - rà. E di can - ti a te sa-

cra - ti o - gni tem - pio suo - ne - rà.

Attila, Act I

"Mentre gonfiarsi l'anima...
Or son liberi I miei sensi!...
Oltre quel limite t'attendo"

Giuseppe Verdi
(1813-1901)

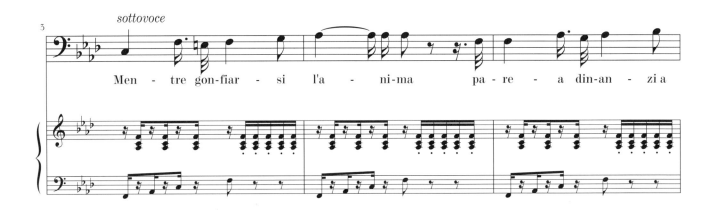

ve - glio, che m'af-fer-rò la chio - ma...

il sen-so eb-b'io tra - vol-to, la man ge-lò sul bran-do; ei mi sor-ri-se in

vol - to, e tal mi fe' co - man-do: Di fla-gel-lar l'in -

car - - co con - tro i mor-ta - li hai

sol:_____ T'ar - re - tra!.. or chiu - so è il var - - co;

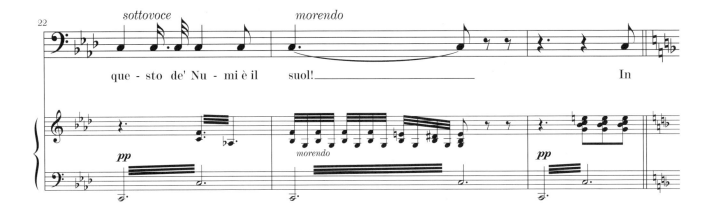

que - sto de' Nu - mi è il suol!_____ In

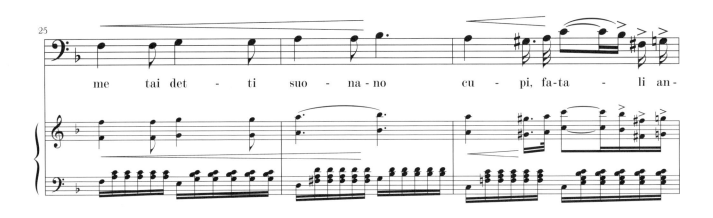

me tai det - ti suo - na - no cu - pi, fa - ta - li an -

cor,_____ e l'al - ma in pet - to ad At - ti - la, in pet - to ad

At - ti-la s'ag-ghiac - cia, s'ag-ghiac - cia, s'ag-ghiac - cia pel ter -

ror, s'agghiac - cia pel ter - ror, e l'al-ma in pet-to ad At-it - la s'ag-ghiac-cia pel ter -

ror:

Allegro ♩ = 126

Or son

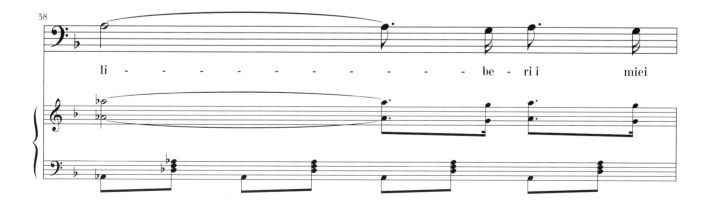

li - - - - - - - - - - be - ri i miei

sen - si! ho - ros - sor_____del mio spa - ven - to. Chia - ma i

dru - i - di, i du - ci, i re. Già più

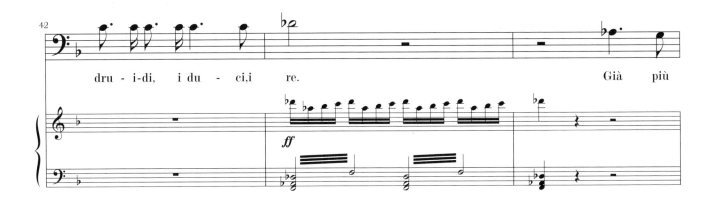

ra - pi - do - del ven - to, Ro - ma i - ni - qua, vo - lo a

te.

Ol - tre quel li - mi-te t'at - ten - do,o

spet - tro! vie - tar - - lo ad At - ti - la_____ chi

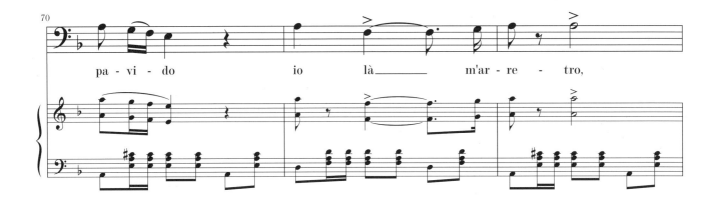

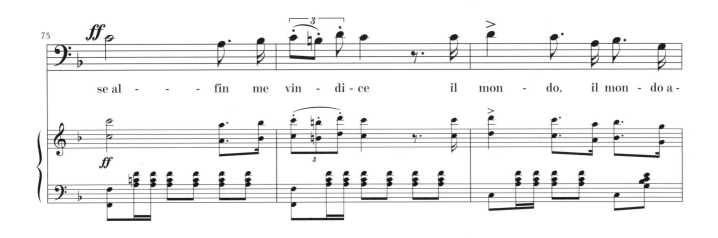

vin - di - ce il mon - do a - vrà, il mon - do a - vrà,_____ il mon - do a -

vrà,_____ se al-fin me vin - - - di-ce il mon-do a - vrà.

Ol - - - tre quel

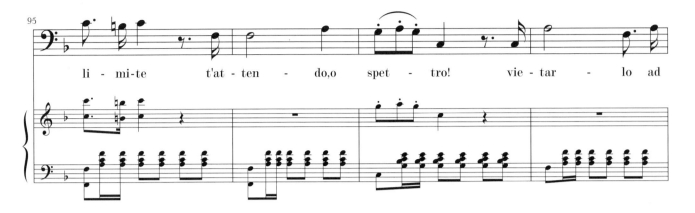

li - mi-te t'at - ten - do,o spet - tro! vie-tar - lo ad

At - it - la_____ chi mai, chi mai po - trà?

ve - drai_____ se pa-vi - do io l'a_____ m'ar - re - tro,

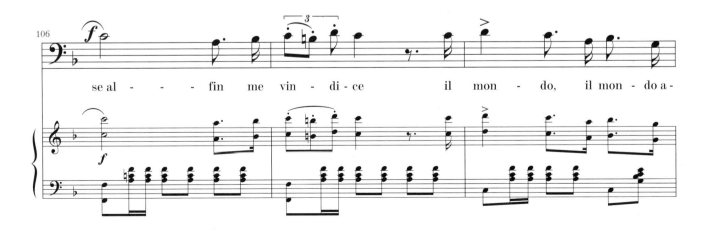

se al - - fin me vin-di-ce il mon - do, il mon-do a-

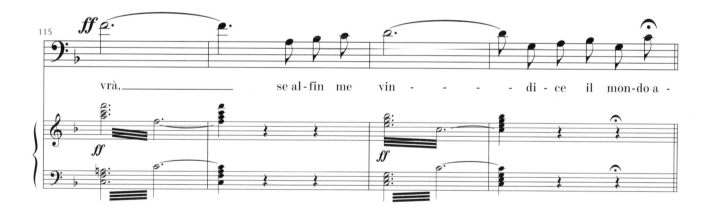

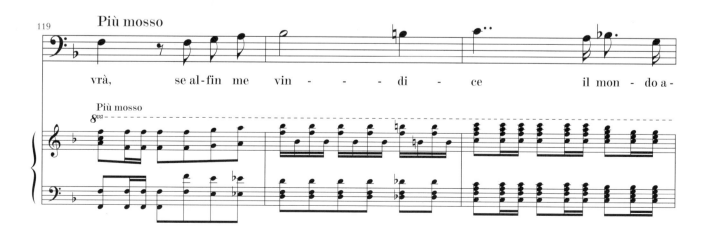

vrà, se al-fin me vin - di - ce il mon - do a-

vrà, a - - vrà, a - - vrà, ah!...

il mon - do, il mon - do a - vrà.

I Vespri Siciliani, Act II
"O patria, o caro patria...
O tu, Palermo"

Giuseppe Verdi
(1813-1901)

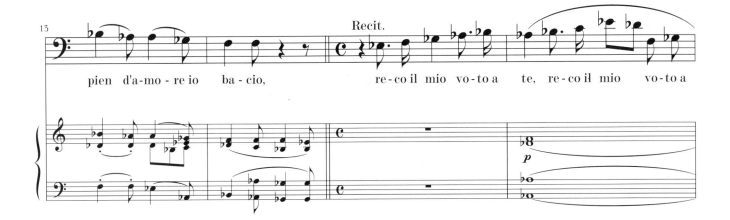

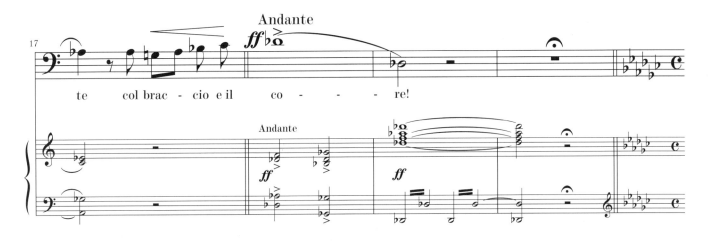

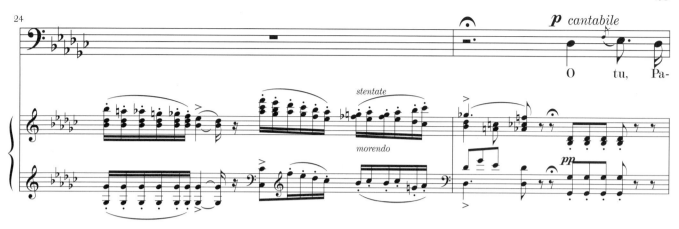

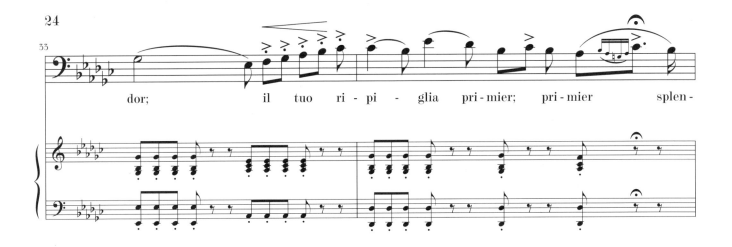

dor; il tuo ri - pi - glia pri - mier; pri - mier splen -

dor! Chie - si ai - ta a stra - nie - re na -

zio - ni, ra - min - gai per ca - stel - la e cit -

tà; ma in - sen - si - bil al fer - vi - do

spro - ne dic - ca cia - scun:

Si - ci - lia - ni, ov' è il pri - sco va - lor?

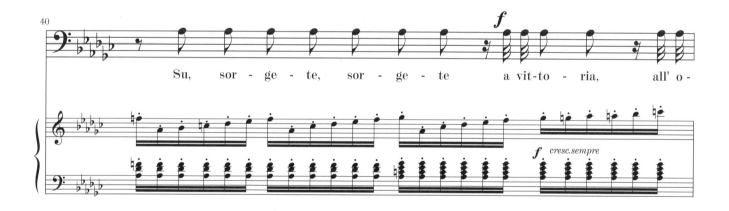

Su, sor - ge - te, sor - ge - te a vit-to - ria, all' o -

nor, a vit-to - - - ria, all' o -

nor, a vit - to - - - ria, all' o -

nor! O tu, Pal - ler - - mo, ter - - ra a - do -

ra - - ta, a me sì ca - ro ri - so d'a -

mor, ah, al - za la fron - - te tan - to ol-trag-

gia - - ta, il tuo ri - pi - glia pri-mier, pri-mier splen-

dor, il tuo ri -

pi - glia, il tuo ri - pi - - - glia al - mo splen -

dor, tor - - - na al pri -

mie - ro, tor - na al pri - mie - - - ro,

ah, tor-na al pri-mie - ro al-mo splen-dor, al-mo splen-

16

dor!

p *morendo*

Introduction and Scene
from "Don Carlo," Act VI
"Ella giammai m'amò...
...Dormirò sol nel manto mio regal"

Giuseppe Verdi
(1813-1901)

El - la giam-mai m'a - mò!　　　no!　　quel cor chiu-so è a -

me a - mor per me non ha, per me non ha!

Io la ri - ve - do an - cor con-tem-plar tri-sta in

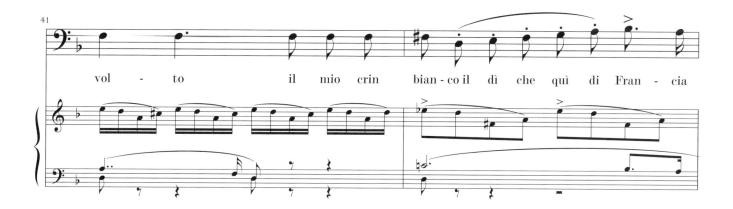

vol - to il mio crin bian - co il dì che quì di Fran - cia

ven - ne.

len - it! il son - no,o Dio, spa - rì da' miei oc - chi lan - guen - - -

ti.   Dor - mi - rò sol nel man-to mio re -

gal, quan - do la mia gior-na-taè giun-ta a se - ra, dor-mi-rò

sol sot - to la vôl-ta ne - ra, dor - mi - rò sot-to la vôl - - ta

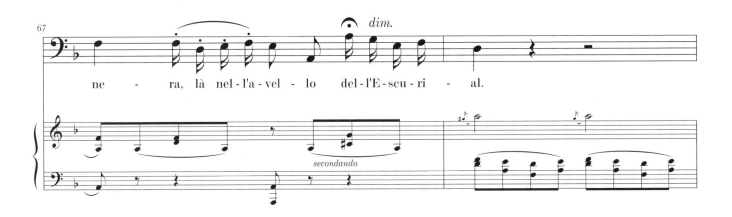

ne - ra, là nel-l'a-vel - lo del-l'E-scu-ri - al.

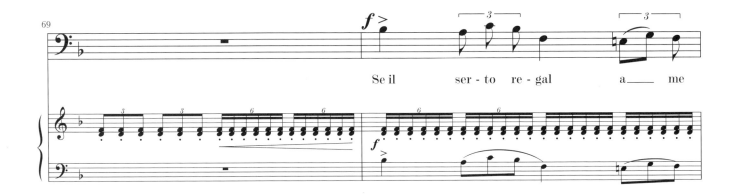

Se il ser - to re-gal a___ me

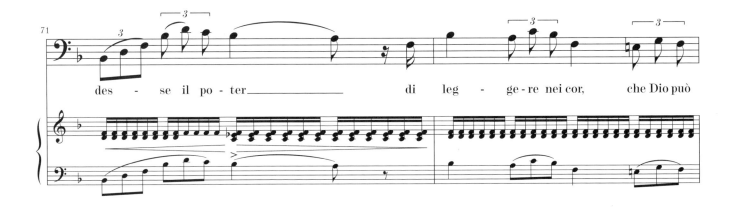

des - se il po - ter___ di leg - ge-re nei cor, che Dio può

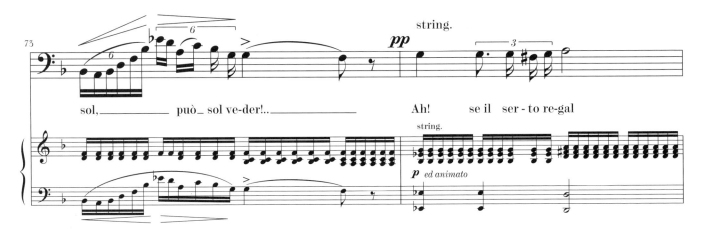

sol,___ può_ sol ve-der!...___ Ah! se il ser - to re-gal

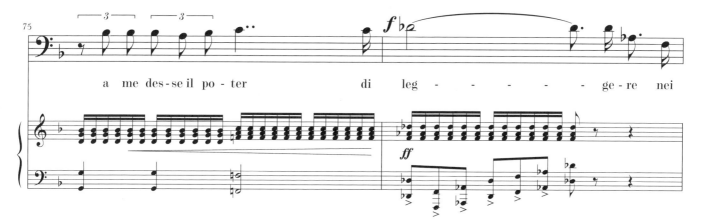

a me des-se il po-ter di leg - - - ge-re nei

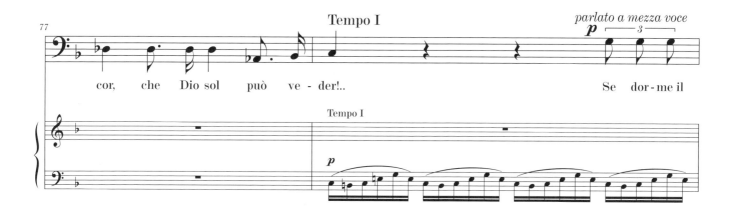

cor, che Dio sol può ve - der!.. Se dor-me il

Tempo I

parlato a mezza voce

Tempo I

pren - ce, ve - glia il tra-di-to - re; il ser - to per - de il

pp

re, il con-sor - te l'o - no - re!

al. Ah! se il ser-to re - gal._____

a me des-se il po-ter di leg - ge-re nei cor!_____

El - la giam-ma i mi a - mò! no! quel cor chiu-so m'è, a-mor per me__ non

ha, a-mor per me non ha!

Engraving: Wiesław Novak

OPERA with ORCHESTRA

Music Minus One is proud to present the finest arias in the operatic repertoire—now available with full orchestral accompaniment! We have brought the finest European vocalists and orchestras together to create an unparalleled experience—giving you the opportunity to sing opera the way it was meant to be performed. All titles are now CD+Graphics encoded so you can see the lyrics on your television screen in real-time—and, as always, the full printed vocal score is included as well.

Bass-Baritone

Bass-Baritone Arias with Orchestra, vol. I
Ivajlo Djourov - Philharmonic Orchestra of Bulgaria/Todorov   MMO CDG 4056
Mozart: Le Nozze di Figaro (The Marriage of Figaro) - Act III: 'Vedrò mentr'io sospiro' (Il Conte); Le Nozze di Figaro (The Marriage of Figaro) - Act I: 'Se vuol ballare, signor contino' (Figaro); **Puccini:** La Bohème - Act IV: 'Vecchia zimarra' (Colline); **Rossini:** Il Barbiere di Siviglia, Act I: 'La callunia è un venticello' (Basilio); **Verdi:** Simon Boccanegra: 'Il lacerato spirito' (Fiesco)

Bass-Baritone Arias with Orchestra, vol. II
Ivajlo Djourov - Plovdiv Philharmonic Orchestra/Todorov   MMO CDG 4066
Beethoven: Fidelio: 'Hat man nicht auch Gold daneben' (Rocco); **Gounod:** Faust: 'Vous qui faites l'endormie' (Mephistopheles); **Mozart:** Le Nozze di Figaro (The Marriage of Figaro) - Act I: 'Non più andrai' (Figaro); Don Giovanni - Act I: 'Madamina! Il catalogo è questo' (Leporello); **Rachmaninov:** Aleko - Act I: Aleko's cavatina (Aleko)

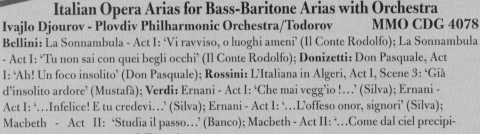

Italian Opera Arias for Bass-Baritone Arias with Orchestra
Ivajlo Djourov - Plovdiv Philharmonic Orchestra/Todorov   MMO CDG 4078
Bellini: La Sonnambula - Act I: 'Vi ravviso, o luoghi ameni' (Il Conte Rodolfo); La Sonnambula - Act I: 'Tu non sai con quei begli occhi' (Il Conte Rodolfo); **Donizetti:** Don Pasquale, Act I: 'Ah! Un foco insolito' (Don Pasquale); **Rossini:** L'Italiana in Algeri, Act I, Scene 3: 'Già d'insolito ardore' (Mustafà); **Verdi:** Ernani - Act I: 'Che mai vegg'io !...' (Silva); Ernani - Act I: '...Infelice! E tu credevi...' (Silva); Ernani - Act I: '...L'offeso onor, signori' (Silva); Macbeth - Act II: 'Studia il passo...' (Banco); Macbeth - Act II: '...Come dal ciel precipita...' (Banco)

Russian Opera Arias for Bass-Baritone
Orlin Anastasov - Orchestra of the Sofia National Opera/Todorov   MMO CDG 4090
Glinka: Ivan Susanin: Susanin's Aria (Susanin); **Mussorgsky:** Prinz Igor: 'Greshno tait...' (Galitzky); **Rachmaninov:** Aleko: 'Volshebnoj Siloj' (Aleko); **Tchaikovsky:** Evgeny Onegin: 'Ljubvi vse vozrasti...' (Gremin); Iolanthe: 'Uje li rokom...' (King Rene)

VERDI Bass-Baritone Arias with Orchestra
Svetozar Rangelov - Orchestra of the Sofia National Opera/Todorov MMO CDG 4078
Attila - Act I: 'Mentre gonfiarsi l'anima' (Attila); I Vespri Siciliani - Act II: 'O patria, o caro patria...O tu, Palermo' (Procida); Don Carlo - Act IV: Introduction & Scene - 'Ella giammai m'amò...Dormirò sol nel manto mio regal' (Philippe); Nabucco - Act II: 'Vieni, o Levita!...' (Zaccaria); Nabucco - Act II: '...Tu sul labbro de veggenti' (Zaccaria)

MUSIC MINUS ONE
50 Executive Boulevard
Elmsford, New York 10523-1325
800-669-7464 (U.S.)/914-592-1188 (International)

www.musicminusone.com
e-mail: mmogroup@musicminusone.com

Printed in Canada